*Wisdom is a living stream, not an icon
preserved in a museum.
Only when we find the spring of
wisdom in our own life can it flow to
future generations.*

Thich Nhat Hanh

Loving Fully

A Love Song

Stephen R. Andrew
Wendy Noyes

Thank you to the New England ATTC at the Brown University School of Public Health for their ongoing support.

Health Education & Training Institute
25 Middle Street
Portland, Maine 04101
www.hetimaine.org

Authors' note

When you want to change and grow, follow this plan for self and others.

RAIN

Recognition, awareness of the trauma whispers and how oppression has impacted your cell structure.

You can be helpful with a heavy dose of empathy and compassion.

Acceptance, the radically acceptance of what has happened to you, pushing aside the historical residue created by your past and ideas and thoughts given to you by others.

You can be helpful with a focus on affirmations.

Investigate what you can do to lean into something differently about your present life and how to move toward your own whisper of hopes and dreams.

You can listen for hopes and dreams; powerful, loving, capable (purpose).

Nurturing, having social capital, a small group of compassionate witnesses who support you as you move gently into the changes of your life.

You can ask them, ask permission, offer ideas.

Love in Action,

Stephen & Wendy

Acknowledgements

We would love to thank dearly people who shaped me both personally and professionally~ Danielle S., Kim A., Doug M., Kelley N., Donna H., Doreen A., Mary C., Brad K., John B., Bob K., Glenn C., Oliver B., Jayme V., Bob J., Linda J., David P., Marie S., Angelina M., Elizabeth M. L., Sarah S., Gabrielle R. T., Jon M., Neil M., Rodney M., Bill M., Terri M., Melissa G., Susan C., David P., Steve B. S., Stefan, Dottie F., Tom C., Dino, friends in the MINT community and all the people in our mutual aid support groups in the last 35 years...all of the donors to our nonprofit, Agape Inc., InnerEdge, and Dignity.

Special thanks to Wendy Noyes for collaborating on this little book.

Hilary, Sebastian, Jeff S. Deborah S., Coral S., Joan A., John P. Robin C., Susan P, Michael P., Blaine H., Christine M., and the Kindred Spirits community.

The human soul doesn't want to be advised or fixed or saved. It simply wants to be witnessed — to be seen, heard and companioned exactly as it is. When we make that kind of deep bow to the soul of a suffering person, our respect reinforces the soul's healing resources, the only resources that can help the sufferer make it through.

Parker Palmer

Loving Fully

Has anybody ever felt fear or pain, experienced toxic shame? Of course, we all have. This book is about Loving Fully and is really about a belief and emotional system, which is several ideas we are playing with in our minds and bodies. Our beliefs are based in our minds, a bunch of thoughts and feelings that we have experienced based upon our past trauma, the cultural messages we have received, and how we perceive them in the moment.

We come into the world with the ability to connect; we need to connect to reduce our own anxiety and fears, and at the same time we want to differentiate, to separate. How do we hold this duality? Most psychology has been developed based on the theories of separation and differentiation; very few focus on connection. In other words, many developmental theories are based on when you separate from the other, the parent or other caregivers. What we are interested in is, "Where is our yearning to connect?" Instead of the "I"ism, where is the "we"ism? In the context of Loving Fully, this book is about not only your own relationships in the world, but also possible relationships you have with every single person, client, patient, consumer, depending on the terminology you want to use (We prefer "people we serve/help"). For every relationship you encounter, at that point in time, you have a choice. The choice is to connect with empathy or to differentiate and fear. Some practices spend a lot of time telling us to consider the possibility of holding the thought in our mind that when we are with somebody that person is either "connecting with us fully or showing us where they have been hurt". That's important because every piece of work we do with every person we serve, every participant we've met has ... Has anybody ever met a defensive individual? What we hold is the possibility that that person is in their hurt, is in their trauma. There is a yearning inside each of us to connect. The further we get into separation, individualization, and isolation, the further we get from connection and the more pain, toxic shame, substance misuse, or other obsessive compulsions arise.

If you want to connect and you are scared, terrified, and afraid to love because of the trauma that happened to you, the hurt that you will experience as you draw inward, the pain of isolation will leave you prone to turn to something for relief, some substance or compulsion to relieve the pain, the hurt.

To love and to be loved. If you don't meet your primary need to love and to be loved then what happens is that you will start going into your trauma whisper. There is something that holds you back and makes you hesitate from this thing called intimacy, from connection. Notice that we do this to protect ourselves from connection which we fear will cause us pain again.

Anxiety

Anxiety is a term we are all too familiar with, whether you're experiencing racing thoughts, rumination, intrusive unwanted thoughts, or maybe you're experiencing a full-blown panic reaction. It has been said many times that people who struggle with anxiety are just simply nice people that tend to want to please people and tend to really place an emphasis on what others think of them!

Whether this is an absolute or not, we tend to feel anxiety in our body due to our overactive bodies and minds; our critical and judgmental minds that create a story; this dialogue that goes on a tangent. Our thoughts can cause us to feel overwhelmed, bad about ourselves, and believers of our thoughts which can cause a multitude of problems! It can be difficult to fully love yourself and others when you feel anxious all the time. People tend to judge themselves harshly and criticize themselves. We see this daily in our own counseling practice. Why are we hardest on ourselves? Why do we want to create an enemy within ourselves? Why do we find it so difficult to love ourselves? If we could only see what others see in us and BELIEVE this. How can others love us and care for us if we don't feel the same way about ourselves? How is it possible that other people can see the loving inside of us? Does this make sense to you? If we told you that all we must do is change our thoughts, would you believe it? It might not be as easy as looking in the mirror once and saying, "I love you." It will take time, like anything, practice, humility, and perseverance. We can change the way we feel about ourselves by changing the way we think. We need to be careful of the words we say to ourselves so we can begin to learn to love ourselves. Once we love ourselves, we can connect to others and feel the true energy connection.

Radical Acceptance

Acceptance is key to a happy mind! Accepting everything as it is will keep our thoughts at ease which equals peace and joy. Now we are not saying that we need to accept abuse of any kind, or people disrespecting us. We are saying to try and accept all the areas of our lives that we cannot control, such as other people's behaviors. This is the one area that people struggle with the most. How many times have we heard, "They made me so mad," "I wish they liked me," "Why do they treat me differently than my brother?" "Ugh, that person just cut me off and I'm going to run them off the road." We know most of us do this every day. We are happier when things go our way and what if we stay happy when things don't go our way? We need to make a conscious effort to not let someone, or something steal our joy. What if we separated from our ego and just noticed what was happening inside our mind? What if we just accepted that we cannot change or control anything outside of us? We cannot control or change people; however, people are so desperate to try to do so because we want people to behave how we expect them to. It's important to let go of the concept that we can control anything except for our thoughts and behaviors.

We can focus on other areas of our lives if we can let go, just let go. We know it's not easy, however we need to train ourselves every day to adjust to a new way of being and thinking. Our mind can be our enemy, or our mind can be our best friend, our greatest lover. Which do you choose?

Awareness

Once we understand and implement this concept that we are aware and begin to practice just being aware of our feelings and thoughts, we can spend more time in the moment instead of spending time in our minds, while our thoughts, in an almost hypnotic pull, wander to our worries, the past, the future, and thoughts of things we cannot control. Awareness works like this. When we are having a negative thought such as, "I am worthless, because no one will talk to me." we can say to ourselves, "I am aware I am having the thought that I am worthless." When we are just aware of our thoughts instead of attaching ourselves to them, we will not provide a belief about the thought. We become separate from our thoughts because we are separate, they are historical residue. Our thoughts are mostly on an unconscious autopilot which creates a thought loop keeping us out of the conscious mind. We want to try to be conscious most of the time, so as not to miss the moment, the life around us. When we think too much, we are missing everything around us! We are, "Lost in thought." Remember, a thought is just a thought until we place meaning behind it. So we need to stop placing meaning behind a meaningless historical thought! We will love ourselves more fully if we practice compassion and empathy towards ourselves and others.

Allowing

What if we allowed people to love us fully and allowed them to come into our lives and trust whatever happens? What if we didn't think about the "What ifs"? We do this because we are trying to control the outcome, which we cannot do. Try it and let us know how it works out! Be in the moment with someone, allow everyone to put your phones down and put away all distractions, allow yourself to take down the walls created by your own historical residue, and allow love and warmth into your heart and body. Allow people to be themselves, and don't be afraid to be yourself. What do you have to lose? We don't want to go through our entire lives and not know what it's like to love fully.

Assisting

When we assist others or contribute to their lives it provides us with a warm feeling, a feeling of helping others and connecting by feeling empathy and compassion. We can contribute to helping others in many forms such as going grocery shopping for a sick friend or volunteering at a soup kitchen or a nursing home. Contributing and assisting is what we all need. Just contributing to the world feels productive; we feel better about ourselves, and we love life more. When you are feeling down, make a list of all the things you can do to assist others. Do something each day for one month, a kind act without getting caught. Assisting others creates a kind and loving world!

Awesome

Yes, YOU are awesome, amazing, kind, and wonderful! Remember this every day and you will succeed if you maintain a focus of kindness. How you feel about yourself determines your love towards others and yourself. Keep a post-it-note with all the nice things about yourself somewhere you see every day to remind yourself just how special you really are, because you really are!

Relationships

If you are in an intimate relationship with a partner, then you might notice that maybe after eight months, ten months, two years, it gets a little troublesome. A few issues come up. Some of us come into relationships bringing a bunch of "stuff" from our past traumas into the relationship. However, we have this great ability to hide it for several months until little by little, we get tired of hiding it because that takes so much work. We start exposing this stuff and the other person goes "ARHHAAGH! AAH! AHH" and then you go "ARHHAAGH! AAH! AHH!" and you both go back and forth like that and the relationship begins dancing apart. "You don't like my stuff (therefore me), do you? Well, I don't like yours, either. I'm going back home (to be safe)!" What I am suggesting to you is that this same thing happens in every relationship you have, whether it be with a client, a participant, or a consumer. Every time you are with somebody, that process, that kind of energy, although subtle, happens within your body. The choice to Love Fully is to decide to look at your own stuff, to look at what it is that you are carrying around in your own mythical baggage.

So, let's imagine that each of us comes into the world with three characteristics, we are born with all three of them. Everybody is universally the same and who you are, in terms of uniqueness, builds off from this core. This is Alice Miller's work *The Drama of the Gifted Child.*

This core is peaceful, clear and untouched. We want you to know that even though you have gotten toxic shame in your life, even though you might feel at times that you are totally inadequate, and we all have, this core, your true self, that part of you that was born lovable, capable, and in connection, wants connection with others.

Isolation and the Deep Yearning to Connect

Whenever you are with any person, the moment that you are with that person there is an opposite going on. Some refer to this as the shadow and the light. We tend to talk about it as the separation and the yearning to deeply connect. The more that you have been wounded, the more that you have been hurt, the more hesitation you will have to connect. We have experienced the desire to connect and at the same time experienced the fear of connecting. When people get closer to us, whether an individual, a family, or group, we get more anxious and uncomfortable. The protective self (the trauma whisper) gets activated.

All those questions start coming up for us, and what is inside of us is the fear of getting close and at the same time an attempt at holding a healthy separation. We are suggesting that connection is a decision which happens in the mind and the heart every moment that you are alive, every moment that you are awake and mindful. When you go to the grocery store today, you will meet someone at the checkout counter. You may not like the way that person is treating you because they are busy and you have a choice in your reaction. If you choose to connect, to stay with them, to be attentive, to empathize, what will happen is that person will likely shift. A smile, a soft eye gaze, a moment of kindness.

Have you noticed that when you put out that gentle energy and focus on a person, they will change their mood. We all have the choice. It's here. It's here now. It is our decision to love and to connect. When we don't make the decision towards connection, some feeling is keeping us from making the conscious decision to connect, to enjoy the magic of connection; the hook where we were injured that created the trauma whisper. The self-protective thoughts which we will call post-traumatic resiliency.

An Unfortunate Culture of "I"ism

What does it mean to love fully? To love means you have the absolute capacity to make the decision every single moment that you are alive to love and that you have the endless potential to love. It means that you do not have some kind of limited ability to love just this person or just that person. In fact, that kind of limited thinking holds us back from developing a community of a "we"ism that will help all of us to heal ourselves. A lot of the social and cultural aspect of addictions, not the biological or the psychological, is based on the "I"ism of our society instead of a "we"ism. We believe that part of the reason that people get well in a 12-step meeting or support group is because of fellowship and community. Not necessarily the specific rules of the fellowship, but that a community in fellowship has figured out ways to develop a ritual so that people feel as safe as possible.

The "we"ism is essential for our being, and as our culture teaches us to compete for success and limited dollars and resources, we separate ourselves away from a "we" and focus on the "I". And the farther we get from holding both of those opposites at the same time, the more addiction we will see in our culture. This is terribly apparent among the Native American population. Between eighty-five and ninety-five percent of the adult males in the Native American population suffer with some form of alcohol or other drug misuse issue. Part of the problem here is that, as a culture, they had a very strong "we"ism and many years of cultural oppression took place to get them not to think about their "we"ism. When you do that to people, they start to feel toxic shame. We are seeing a resurgence of Native American thinking in this country because we have a desperate need to think about how to develop ourselves as a culture of connection, to awaken their core self to operate with their own social capital.

Our country's children, adolescents, and teenagers are getting more and more involved in substance misuse has something to do with the fact that their "we"ism is based only on their own age-limited culture. They don't have the skills to develop their own cultures without mentors, young adults, and older adults and people who can enter that culture and let them have respect, honor, and so on and give them a way to get out of oppression. Since they develop it by themselves, they develop it in such a way as to be deviant as seen by adults to fill a need. Once you get into that culture you find that they don't have a need for isolation, they have a need for connection, a "we"ism, and once they have a reason to take a direction towards self care, they normally take that direction to connect. You can look at any group of people, especially an oppressed group of people, and see that they will develop toward themselves. Why? Because we all have a desperate need to connect and to feel the journey, the vulnerability to be loved and love to be safe.

Capability

We came into the world powerful, lovable, capable, and wanting to belong. We have the capacity to love way beyond our abilities. We have capabilities way beyond what we could ever imagine. The only thing that holds us back from taking on the things in life that we really want to do is to step toward a new relationship, a new job, going back to school. The only thing that holds you back is your limited beliefs, it is not your capabilities. Well, you might think, "I'm stupid, I can't go to school." There are thousands of young people in our culture, and they believe that notion, what they believe and hear in their heads is that they are not smart enough. Some of you believe that you are not smart enough. Thoughts like these hold us back and limit the capability that we have. If you want to spend the time and the attention, we could figure out some of the incredible questions that this society is holding itself with, for instance, how to hold all the diversity in this nation. It is estimated that we use six percent of our brain capacity, it may be two or three percent at times, but six percent on a good day. However, what if we used ten percent? What if we used twenty? What if we focused ourselves that well? Somehow, we believe that something holds us back. That something is our toxic shame that has gathered as we passed through our developmental stages, often the early ones where trauma and oppression begins.

Clean and Clear Relationships

There are people we need to talk to in our lives to clear up our relationships with, yet we hold back out of fear and shame. We don't say what we need to say to them. Think about that for a moment; because as you sit here right now there is probably somebody in your mind who you haven't reached out to in a while for some reason, and in some way, it's a fear. You are absolutely capable of having clean and clear relationships. You are absolutely loving, and you say, "What about them?" Remember, you are absolutely capable of having clean and clear relationships. There is the holding of the opposites. There is the separation that makes you unique. We want you to imagine that in the connection there is this sense of compassion and empathy. When you are with someone, you make a decision to really know, on an affect level, who they really are. Empathy has multiple levels to it. Imagine that you can have that affect level and at the same time know that you are a separate human being. You almost can feel that you are in the skin, in the soul of the other person. Try to have that much curiosity about that other person's life. During the time that you are with them, try to really want to know what makes them think, feel, and hope for. Now that is powerful empathy. At the same time, your mind knows that you are a separate human being. If we were to make a conscious decision to hold that kind of empathy in every one of our relationships rather than spilling out in our heads the ideas of what we want to happen or even worry about how they see you, we would be so much better off. Remember, let go of the outcome. The issue of boundaries naturally comes if you hold one part of your brain in your own separateness and uniqueness. If you can hold an empathy affect about that individual and another part of you not worrying about them, you'll see it in your thinking, you're not worrying about them. You know you are separate at the same time you can still connect with the energy and heart of that human being.

We say energy, because emotion is what we are usually working with. Emotion is a beautiful word, because it says "E-motion," energy in motion. When you are with another person you can feel their energy. You want your sharing with another to get the clogs out of your brain and heart long enough to feel the energy and realize at the same time that you are a separate human being by letting go of the outcome. That is having good, healthy, compassionate boundaries.

Fitness

If each one of us decides today to become a marathon runner, we don't just go out and do it. We start slowly and work at it. Empathy and compassion and feelings and emotions are just like our physical selves, we need to exercise them. We ought to exercise them through listening deeply. What happens is, in this magic connection, in this core where you are always powerful, always capable, always lovable, and, finally, you want and desire and have a yearning to connect with every human being you come into contact with when you notice it. Then what happens is, stuff lays on top. What's that stuff? What lies on top of this gorgeous jewel of your true self? Let's call it "mud." Imagine that there are layers upon layers of this mud that has developed over the years (trauma and oppression). Some of us have grown up in families where there has been a lot of trauma, like ourselves, or where communication wasn't clear. Some of us were raised in a culture where we received messages such as, "If you are a male you shouldn't cry." or, "If you are a female you shouldn't get angry." Some of us were poor and learned to hoard money. Some of us learned to fritter away money because we were afraid of the energy. Some of us have issues of power and control, aggression and passivity.

So, what happens in this context is that we hold that mud around our true selves, and what then happens to our communication is that it comes bouncing out of that stuff. Anybody noticed that when we speak to somebody sometimes it isn't very clean? It is bouncing out of all of the layers of that stuff and ends up coming out poorly, differently than you really wanted it to sound. What happens is that mud is your own journey to figure out. "Hmm, every time we walk that way there is this peculiar sound." So, what happens is that you must figure out where you were hurt in the process of laying all that mud down and allow yourself to experience and know what you think and feel about it. One of the things we have done is we have developed a culture that doesn't place a lot of emphasis on feeling our feelings. We think that is part of the problem. A helper is an emotional trainer, someone who will let you talk and experience the feeling of being heard, believed, seen, and valued so that you can learn how to experience self-empathy. A big part of the work is allowing people to move the energy that is in their body out so they can see that core again and again. They will practice with you and they will begin to learn to maneuver through and peel off the mud. That is honorable work, folks. Even if we don't want to deal with our emotions, we still have those feelings. Those feelings are still there, and we all need to be able to deal with them and work through them and discharge them as positive energy to pursue our hopes and dreams.

The Fire Alarm Theory

If the culture takes away your anger, it also takes away the emotion of change. Anger and frustration were given to us as the energy towards change and are where our passion, our drive, and our advocacy comes from. That's where we know and believe we can change things. That energy, that frustration, needs to be there for us to change our lives. Sadness is a place where we are allowed to let go of our energy, to release, to grieve. Fear is a place of warning, a signal that you are not safe. It's kind of like a fire alarm. If you have had a lot of hurt in your life you will tend to respond to that warning a lot more quickly; fear dominates those who are reactive. Can you imagine growing up in a place where the fire alarm was going off all the time? If you grew up in a family or community like that, what happens is that you can't trust your fear, your own alarm system, anymore so you shut down and become depressed or very anxious. If you have the type of fire alarm that, when the batteries start going dead, you hear "ERRRR! ERRRR! ERRRR!". We are not the kind of people who immediately go to the store. We are more the kind who take the alarm apart and forget to go to the store, or create external softness. That's like our fear and anxiety. Our batteries run out because we have constantly been bombarded with a lack of safe interactions and our fear, our defense, no longer works for us. We pull out the battery and it doesn't work for us anymore. Fear is a valuable emotion for warning, if we let it work properly. We do not listen with gentleness or we listen and consider it absolute truth. How do we know the difference?

Joy Droppings

Anger is a wonderful emotion for the possibility of change. Sadness is an emotion of letting yourself feel the grief and the pain and the hurt from your life. Shame is a wonder too. It helps us define what's right and wrong, and creates a moral compass we need and is not always toxic. It's a way of deciding what's right and wrong to help us define our place in the universe, our separation, our spiritual morality. And then there is joy and happiness and all of the emotions that go along with the excitement of courage, of taking a risk, stepping into the unknown. They are there to remind us to celebrate our bravery. For instance, do you spend time starting things? Are there books laying around with bookmarks, they kind of have the "wing" look to them from laying open on a table for so long? And how about those undone projects around the house, the ones that have either been started or at least thought about, but that's all? You know, the lack of completion in our lives. Have you ever noticed that when you have successfully gone from an intention to a completion of a chore, an idea you get a little smile? When you finally finish one book you think "Yeah!" It's a happy feeling! What you get are little internal joy droppings. Oh, the image that conjures! You get these little joy droppings and they go "blip, blip, blip" and hit this place called your self-worth, your true self, your core yearnings. That is where you push off the mud.

Angel Training

If you approach every single person as having the same yearning to love well, to connect as you do, if you approach them as though they have full self-esteem, then what happens is that the only thing we need to do is be empathetic and compassionate to allow the discharge of the historical residues to move the mud. The safety of skillful empathy and compassion. You are in charge of every relationship you have from now on, you can no longer decide to blame somebody else, "They are resistant. They are in denial. They have too many defense mechanisms." These are all ways of giving ourselves permission to get out of the relationship. These are all just terms. Of course, people are in denial. Of course, people are resistant or they put up defense mechanisms. If you were given that trauma, that history, you would be too. If you weren't you'd be gone ... something may have snapped in you a long time ago. All we are saying is be kind and love every individual you meet. If we decide from now on---did you know it takes four adults to raise every child? It also takes compassionate witnesses in your life to tap into your motivation to be powerful, loveable, and capable, to give a purpose and desire for connectedness. Our culture is going the other way. Sometimes It takes many adults to raise a child. Why? Because we can't always be in a frame of mind to connect, we are "hooked". When a child can't connect with me because I am tired, hurt, angry, hungry, or lonely, the child can move to someone else to get their needs met. That tells them that they are seen, heard, beloved, and valued. What happens otherwise is that the adult has to either bracket feelings and throw them out and push the child away, abandon their needs or engulf them. What we need is for all of us to choose to be "angels" in young people's lives. There is an incredible amount of research that says that the presence of a nurturing adult in a young person's life is the true criteria to resiliency. This means that if you can remember and practice it, every person and young person who crosses your path will have an opportunity to be inspired.

We have done an informal study of hundreds of people who have come through our offices and we have been fortunate enough to do workshops across the country and have talked with all kinds of people. Everyone who is alive and working on their discovery recovery, working on who they are, and stepping through their fears and trauma whispers are taking all kinds of risks, are all leaning into courage. They have one criteria which is the same for all of them; they met a person who believes in them who created an atmosphere of radical acceptance along the way. They met an angel, somebody outside of their family who cared enough to help them sneak through the mud and get to the core. And you know what? It doesn't take very long. It doesn't have to be a professional, just someone skillful. What we need is the support of others and to make the commitment to "love fully" (This is "Angel Training").

Scared of Being Too Powerful

We have been caught in our story, our history. As a culture, we know what has hurt us, what has covered us in mud. We hold it up and say, "This is my story, my historical residue. This is why I can't get close." This is what creates our defensiveness, our pesky ego. You are responsible to make the decision to "love fully" every moment you are alive. You have to choose, sometimes every thirty seconds. We know this can be very difficult and challenging, but with support from the right people we can make that decision. You pull out your story, you look at it and recognize the energy you are willing to discharge in a conscious dialogue with others. This moves the energy so that you can be available to embrace the vulnerability of the whisper of your hopes and dreams.

If you just hold your story up and say, "I can't do it." that limited thinking keeps you safe but holds you back. It's thinking like that that holds an entire nation back. One of the things that Nelson Mandela said during his inaugural address that was so powerful was, "We are not scared of being inadequate, we are scared of being powerful."

What if we had it? What if there was nothing really wrong with you? We realize that people who write self-help books would be out of business, and the truth is, there is nothing wrong. The only thing that is holding us back is the belief that we don't matter, that we are not loveable, and that the world is not to be trusted. What if we were so powerful that together this small group of people could actually change the Congress of the United States so that they embraced acceptance and compassion? Remember they are only in their hurt, their trauma. And they are. If you listen to them, it is usually some kind of a story about pain and toxic shame.

The bottom line is that we are not inadequate in any way. We might say that we are as a great excuse to keep from having to do the "work". If you are not able to "love fully" in the moment, then something is blocking you, holding you back. You have the responsibility (which, by the way, is a beautiful word, it means that you have the ability to respond empathetically, to set boundaries with kindness) you have the responsibility to move that blockage and be in a skillful conscious dialogue.

On Dialogue

Let me just say something about dialogue. Dialogue is to love as the blood is to the body. Now, if you could imagine what would happen if you stopped the cyclic process of moving your blood throughout your body? You would be dead. Now if you are not in conscious dialogue with people then you are dead on an emotional level. One is on a physical level, and the other is on an emotional level. We are and can and ought to be, from a holistic perspective, on an emotional sobriety training program to get our conversation going and to keep it going. What happens in dialogue is that the two of us are exchanging energy. Just like on a treadmill in the physical exercise program, we are moving energy. As we move compassionate energy, we are connecting with each other, experiencing each other. As we are connecting with each other there is a part of your being that starts producing these little "joy droppings". As you stay in that dialogue, you drift down through the layers of feelings, down through the layers of mud, and eventually you get to your true core self. Sometimes you get just a glimpse of that true self. "God grant me serenity". Sometimes you get it during a moment of calmness. Your goal is to then make it two moments and then three moments. Start taking those moments and sewing them together. Maybe you get one, and then it's a week later before you get another one, but then it's only two hours before you get the next. Wherever your journey is leading you, your goal is to lean into those moments and make the most of them. Allow yourself that level of dialogue. You see, just like when the flow of blood stops, the body dies; when communication stops, love dies and resentment and separation are born. Conscious skillful dialogue can restore a dying relationship.

A metaphor. If you are not feeling well, you start taking better care of yourself physically. You may start in an on-going fitness routine, pay more attention to what you are eating, maybe start meditating daily, and you slowly begin to feel better. The same is true with your emotional sobriety. You start to create conscious skillful dialogue. When you are with somebody and they show some resistance to connecting with you, that resistance is their fear, their trauma whisper. Your "work" is to figure out a soft way, with compassion and empathy, to continue to stay with them so that the energy begins to move. Really, all the "pesky" ego psychology, all of the self-psychology, all of the psychodynamics, all of the training, it is all about the process. They are all looking, from different angles, at moving the dialogue and the energy so that people can say their truth without shame or blame.

We are not advocating for you to, as a reflex, advise or attempt to change someone. The advice we give tends to hold back the dialogue. When we think we have the answer and we give it, the dialogue stops. What if we believed that people already know, or have the powerful capacity to ask for more help than they are comfortable with? The difference for people getting to their dreams would simply be that they need more time because there is still mud in the way. We are all capable of figuring it out or deciding for ourselves. Instead, we get in there and begin to give them advice because in some way it makes us feel "good". Now some helpers will say, "That's what I'm paid to do." You are in this to move the energy, you are an emotional sobriety trainer, your role is to get it moving in a healthy way. Your role is to get the conscious dialogue moving in every avenue of your life: with your children, with your spouse, your lover, your partner, your small cadre of friends, with those around you as well as with those you see professionally. It's crazy, but it gets more difficult with those who you care deeply for. This makes sense if you think that if you are way out there, you send out all this energy freely because you have all of this space to hold us. If someone is close to us, we start to get scared. The fear starts coming up because we become afraid of abandonment, of losing our power, of our historical residue and our toxic shame. Below all of those layers is our forgiveness and love. If you want to know how to forgive someone who has hurt you in your life, you do need to not get them to change, you need to go through the layers of your own mud through conscious dialogue with them and others. If you want to "love fully" somebody who has hurt you, then you need to drift through your hurt, your anger, your resentment, and then you can come to a radical acceptance that they were doing the best that they could at that time with the resources they had. It's not about them doing something, it's about you doing something. It is you taking full responsibility to "love fully" in your life.

The Car Wash

Our premise is that you can learn to wash off the mud and as that happens, your communications will become clearer and clearer.

"So, you say that people come into this world empty and our work is to help them, in some way, to be a member of their cadre, to support them as they move along in life and to help them develop the skills of empathy, compassion, boundaries with kindness, and heartfelt apologies to help them get through to the next growth process."

We understand where others are coming from, we are all the same. I hold the belief that people really do come into the world and that what happens to them is that they are never damaged but essentially things happen to each of us. What happens is that today, before the day is over, somebody is going to sling some mud, some judgment at each of us. But, we have the ability to be a car wash. We can figure out a way to get rid of that mud. We can hold up a shield and catch it, and in that way keep it from hitting our soul and not letting it into my core self. We build the shield with the belief that people are loving me fully and showing me where they have been holding onto their mud. We could end up with it on our core selves and when that happens, our critic starts to show. Does anybody have a critic in their head? The critic starts to say things like, "You know you really didn't do a good job." or, "You aren't really organized." These thoughts and others start to go around in our heads as our critics start to engage with us. You hear the trauma whispers echoing: "I don't matter, I am not loveable, the world is not to be trusted". The bottom line is, I am suggesting that we can work with those whispers and, in fact, the next level of empathy is self-empathy, and that we gain self-empathy by giving away empathy to others. The hardest part is to actually decide to be our own car wash, so that when that mud comes, you can hold it in such a way that you begin to hold it outside of yourself, to look at it, and to see how much truth there is in it. See how much value it has for you. It is very important, for me, to hold it outside of myself and decide whether it's worth bringing in and doing some work with it and allowing the conscious dialogue to continue, or to just drop it and leave it. I hold dear this old phrase, "If it walks like a duck and talks like a duck, it's probably a duck."

So, if we hear something more than once, we tend to hold that even closer, and the more we hear something, the more we are willing to play in the mud. I have a philosophy that goes along with a Rick Charette song, I Love Mud. The lyrics are, "I am absolutely, positively wild about mud." What that means is that we are not scared of taking on the stuff that people bring in our direction. We can hold it out here, not trying to avoid it, and make sure that it is allowed to come so that we can hold it, see it, feel it and not try to knock it away the minute it comes, but to really hold it. That's a hesitation that people need from us to really listen to them deeply.

We don't hold that we are empty vessels when we are born. We hold that we are all lovable, capable, connected, and wanting to connect. There is a connection that comes automatically during the early first stages of life, the immediate infant's attachment bond. We all come into the world with a yearning to connect. We all have it. We do not know a separation; we get that over time. We hold the two opposites. We have a need for the duality of separation or differentiation and for connection, and the connection is a core yearning. The more you are unable to connect in this world, the more trauma and oppression you experience, the more likely that you will not be able to see or experience your own lovable and capable self. A lot of theorists hold that addictions and compulsions are about doing something so you can't feel it anymore. You can't feel that core yearning anymore so you shut down. Once you've shut down, how far can that go? Can it go all the way to psychosis? Is that what a dissociative disorder is? Is suicide a possibility when you cannot connect with another human being and can't see any other way out? Is this the place for the protective factor of helplessness? Is depression really the lack of connection and too much negative self-talk? What we have found over and over and over is that if you lack connection, if you can't feel the connection and love with other human beings, then you will become depressed and isolated from others.

Depression can be a Beautiful Word

Now, depression is a very beautiful word. It's just like it sounds, to hold the energy inside, to keep it down so that it can't move. What happens is that the anger that is held down is focused inward, is the depression. Well, it's more than anger, it's anger and hurt and fear and toxic shame. It's all of the toxic emotions going inward. It's like some kind of a manhole cover that is holding the energy in this giant container called emotional sobriety.

How many of us have heard a message in our culture that says, in some way, that we should not show our emotions, we should not let our energy out? In a simple way, women and girls are taught to hold onto their trauma. Men are taught to only feel anger as a way to injure others to create isolation and loneliness. There are so many messages, obvious everywhere, on soap operas, at work, in magazines, on the news, in our religious institutions that say we should not feel or that we should not show the way we feel. "It's okay to have play and joy, but don't have the other emotions." Let us tell you, you cannot have play and joy without the other emotions. Energy is energy, you can't tap into one part of the energy and not tap into all of it. So instead of dealing with pain, many of us will cut off the joy.

"So why should we want to experience the pain, the hurt? Must we experience this energy and these hurts in our bodies?" Well, if you don't let go, you'll never experience the joy in life. Whatever level of energy you are willing to experience with other people in your conscious dialogue, whatever level you are willing to empathize with others, that is the level to which you will experience joy in your life.

If a person comes into your life and they are experiencing a lot of emotional turmoil and you are not able to be with them, you will send them a subtle message that they should stop because you are not willing to drift down. We often think of being a helper as putting some sort of rope around ourselves and drifting down into people's energy and just letting them drift right through their sadness, their anger, their toxic shame, their love, and their joy. We've got this little thing as helpers, and we are just doing my best to stay out of their stuff. Our energy is there to somehow keep them going, using empathy and compassion, to help them reveal their hurts. What would it look like if you were in a relationship where there was this mutuality, this power with? Mutuality is a very beautiful word.

It means not having more power than another. The beauty of what's happening to us in relationships and in our culture is that the power differential is moving and that we can't have these kinds of power relationships anymore. We have moved from power over to power with. People are asking for shared power. What they are looking for when they become involved in gangs and cultures and so on and so forth is because they feel that they deserve shared power and are getting instead lots of power over. Well, if they aren't getting it from one place, they will go somewhere where they feel like they are in mutuality. There are kids out there saying to others, "You either give it to me or I'll kill you." It is just that simple. It's about power, and the human soul craves power with. As long as people feel "oppressed" in our culture they are going to search for power; and if they cannot get it directly, and there are no means of getting it directly from our culture, then they will resort to a violence, internal or external. The issue is about mutuality. What will it take for us, then, to be culturally diverse enough so that we can be in mutually empowering relationships?

We need to extend our energy and become a positive influence in other people's lives, maybe become an angel. A very powerful young man grew up in a very violent household. He has two brothers who have committed suicide and died. Two brothers out of five, and the other two are alcoholic. He is the only one out of five brothers who has done something with himself. He is a schoolteacher, he's doing well. Why? How did you make it? His answer was, "Mr. Proctor (the name has been changed), Mr. Proctor next door took me outdoors on his tractor. He would do it often, and when my father was drunk or mad and said I couldn't go, Mr. Proctor would convince my father that it was okay. He would take me on vacations" This young man told this story so beautifully, so elaborately that we can feel the intensity, the energy, the hurt of what it must have been like to grow up in that type of environment. At the same time, we can feel the power of him being pulled out of the hurt, the trauma. The power of him being told over and over again that he was important, that he mattered. Being told that he was important saved his life. What do you think Mr. Proctor did for a living? He was a schoolteacher. We mimic what we like, we mimic what we see when we feel heard, believed, valued and seen. What we are suggesting to you is that, as these families become more and more entangled in marital discord and trauma, what happens is that these young people need more and more emotional support.

Be Curious

We should come to each conversation from a place of curiosity. What is it that we need to know? Multiculturalism, for instance, is a powerful force in this culture. Bring an attitude of an ally. What is it like to be you? You may not know what it is like to be a different color than you are in this country; you may not know what it's like to be a man or a woman. If you are curious and hold a third eye for what it might be like to be another with empathy and compassion and at the same time knowing your separation. That's what we need with multiculturalism. This commitment to the context of curiosity of the issues of our time. People need to be seen, heard, believed, and valued. How do you see this moment in time? How do you see the future? How do you see power or resources? How do you see things through your vision of the global community? Do you care enough to have that curiosity? If we are in mutuality, we will be curious. If you are in a relationship with another human being, you need to have some kind of curiosity about what they are like, what their story is for them. It may be hard to do. You might put a layer of your mud on top of the relationship by thinking that you know what they are like, by not being curious. Thinking that you know what they are like throws on a layer and when you throw on the layer you miss the mutuality. By throwing on that layer, you have decided that you are a little more powerful, you re-traumatize the original hurts. At that moment you have decided that you have the power. Your role is to be humble with another and be skillful in your conversation.

Spontaneity

We need to say them with something spontaneous and meaningful. What we have learned from that process of being with people is that we are using the same belief system every time we are with another human being. What we do is to spend some time and ask them to spontaneously risk the way they think and feel. We want to get some idea of what is going on in their head and heart. Every time that you are sitting with somebody and are doing something in your thinking, you may not be increasing the connection. There is a critic and there is a nurturing voice of hopes and dreams. That is the voice of self-empathy, a belief in yourself. Your intention is to see to it that the relationship is authentic, spontaneous, and at the same time, self-nurturing. That it has to have some self-empathy to nurture the movement towards hopes and dreams.

Freedom of Movement

With most of the people we help, we find that they have been hurt and are suffering in some way and they may hold their body in a rigid way. The more that they have been hurt the more that their body is tight. If there were mutuality, there would be freedom of movement. Your hands would be relaxed, your muscles would be loose, you would dance like a crazy person. Respectful mutuality creates a chemical reaction that serves as a relaxation medication.

Persistence

We want you to remember that we will be your cadre; we will persist. Persistence is a part of mutuality. When you are in a relationship with another person you want to have the attitude of persistence and tenacity. Those particular characteristics will help you stick with it and be successful. This works with others. The issue is the conscious dialogue. Can we have the dialogue to change the conditions that promote trauma, oppression, and stigma? Can we keep the messaging going? Persistence.

Be Humble!

We also have to have this piece called humility, as partners, friends, lovers, and as helpers. We have it all of the time, every time we get in front of any audience. We have the potential to really look foolish right now, and that's the chance we are willing to take. We ask you to have that same willingness to be humble, to decide that, whatever it is, when you take that step into the unknown, know that something is going to happen. It may not be exactly what you want, and allow the risk to be your teacher. There is a part of the darkness that none of us knows. Please lean into it. Be open to it. Let the process humble you. You have no idea what it will be so be curious. Let go of the notion that you have to control it and have an attitude of, "Bring it on". The most important thing we have to say about humility is that most of us are hanging onto control for dear life. It's okay to keep some control, and you need to have humility mixed into the soup. You have to be able to hold both of those dualities at the same time. And you have to be willing to hold humility with the intention to connect skillfully with another.

Playfulness

You also need to have a sense of humor and playfulness. That playfulness comes from within yourself.

There is the critic that is the super pesky ego, a place within that tells us whether we did right or wrong, the judgment whisper of toxic shame and the nurturing voice of self-empathy that helps us be courageous. We need to work with this duality. Most of the people that we see in our practice are struggling with the critic in their head which says that they are not good enough, that they are inadequate. What most of us need is to learn to listen to the whisper of our self-empathetic voice, a voice with a child-like quality. The more child-like you can be in your body and in your spirit, the more you can allow that quality to be your uniqueness. You want to have fun, you want to play, you want to be spontaneous. Do it. If you grew up in an atmosphere where you couldn't have that because it wasn't safe, then you may have to literally make a conscious decision to go out and learn how to play. Show up to workshops and classes and places where you can develop your play; be outrageous and push yourself to the edge of being comfortable. As you learn how to do that, you may work through the mud on the places where you held yourself back. If you find that you are, or you are helping with, a person who doesn't have a lot of humility, then take more risks, with empathy. Push through the mud. If you find yourself with a person who doesn't have a lot of humor, then you have to make the conscious decision to be more humorous and find a way to push that energy out so that there is more energy in your life. Laughter is a discharge of the hurt, of the mud. You may have to learn how to tell really bad jokes. You may have to make an effort to take time to be with people and have some belly laughs. If you can get the endorphins and the chemistry flowing through laughter, you will gain back your healing ability and your wholeness. Just that one track alone will help a lot. The theory is that there was not much humor as we were growing up, there wasn't much that was funny, so the funny was taken out of us. So go rent a silly video or do something outrageous. At first, you'll feel uncomfortable, you will feel awkward. Tell your cadre of compassionate witnesses, hold onto that awkwardness, and go for it. If you practice long enough, it will turn into a new behavior. And you have got to be willing to hold the awkwardness, be willing and open to change. Wherever you are in your life right now, keep the momentum moving forward. Recovery and discovery are terms that encompass finding or creating that part of you that is spontaneous, zestful, lovable, capable, powerful, and connected to your natural self. Be open to change, take risks, be willing to go out into the unknown, take on something new, clear up those old relationships, make amends, decide to be, strive to be in a win-win relationship with everyone. There is no one you need to blame for where you are at the present time. Your only intention is to connect deeply with another human being in order to have a win-win relationship with them.

Most relationships are stuck in a win-lose. If you are stuck in a relationship with another where you feel conflict, it is usually a win-lose. You have an opinion and they have an opinion. The bottom line is that you both have an opinion and it can be held. You can figure out a way to have win-win, we are capable of having win-win situations. If you think that person is not good enough because they are the ones who are not making this happen, then you are giving up your power. If you are doing this, you are giving the power of the situation away instead of empowering yourself. Hold the duality; I am powerful and I am loving fully. There is connection and separation, there is humility and confidence, there is light and darkness, you can hold all of these. Your intention is to allow the two opposites of your being, the heart and the head, to be in different places. It feels confusing, it feels awkward, and allow it to be, with great compassion. Allow it to be because in that process you will be able to be who you are in a natural way.

"Loving fully" is a decision. It is a decision that you can make with every person along the way. We once did this workshop around "Loving Fully" and at lunch we all went together to this ice cream shop and we beamed all this loving attention to this poor person who was trying to serve the ice cream.

We want to kind of remind you before we come to the end of this crazy book that the most important work there is in the human kind is helping another. What you are doing is very, very important. You won't always be appreciated. Don't look for the kudos, just be the angel. This is vital work, supporting and helping.

It is vital what we ask you to do.

What is Success?

To laugh often and much:

*To win the respect of intelligent people
and the affection of children,*

*To earn the appreciation of honest critics
and endure the betrayal of false friends;*

To appreciate beauty,

To find the best in others,

*To leave the world a bit better whether by
a healthy child, a garden patch, or a
redeemed social condition;*

*To know even one life has breathed easier
because you lived.*

This is to have succeeded.

Ralph Waldo Emerson

Stephen R. Andrew LCSW, LADC, CCS is a storyteller, consultant, community organizer and trainer who maintains a compassion-focused private practice and facilitates weekly men's, coed, and Motivational Interviewing learning groups. He provides coaching and training domestically and internationally for social service agencies, health care providers, substance abuse counselors, criminal justice, and other groups. Stephen lives in Portland, Maine with his sweet wife Hilary, and is the proud father of Sebastian.

Wendy Beth Noyes, LCPC is a Licensed Clinical Professional Counselor. She has a Bachelors in Psychology, and a Masters in Mental Health Counseling with a Forensic Concentration. She has a private practice in Maine and is passionate about teaching people ways to cope with their struggles in life. Wendy enjoys reading and researching new ways to cope with symptoms that individuals struggle with. Wendy has gone through many trainings on trauma, anxiety, and Energy Psychology. Wendy is also currently writing another book that will be out by the Spring of 2024.

Making it happen is our commitment to the world ~50% of our profits will go to the (not- for- profit), AGAPE Inc., dedicated to providing support services and education to create compassionate solutions that strengthen our communities.

www.dignitymaine.com